CREDIT REPAIR SECRETS

THE BEST TRICKS AND SECRETS TO CHANGE YOUR FINANCIAL LIFE. REPAIR YOUR CREDIT, IMPROVE YOUR SCORE. MANAGE YOUR EXPENSES AND MONEY SIMPLY AND EFFECTIVELY IN TIME OF CRISIS.

WARREN MOORE

TABLE OF CONTENTS

INTRODUCTION

You may have heard that bad credit repair is impossible or illegal. A bad credit report can be repaired. If you contact a law firm that specializes in repairing a credit report, the entirety of this should be possible legitimately. If you contract an organization that isn't a law office, it might be accomplishing something inadequate or illicit. The only way to be sure that the credit repair information you receive is legal, accurate and effective is to contact a lawyer.

NOT ALL LAWYERS SPECIALIZE IN REPAIRING BAD DEBT REPORTS.

Those who typically charge an initial advisory fee and a monthly fee offer a company, Lexington Law, the reimbursement of overpayments if they are unable to remove a significant amount of negative credit report information. Some companies calculate credit repair information and provide useful tips. Where do you get your credit report from? How to write a letter and

other credit repair information that you can find for free. These and companies that claim they can do bad credit repair in less than 30 days should be avoided.

Regardless of whether it is called "problematic", "less than perfect" or simply "bad credit", anyone with a rating lower than 680 can benefit from poor credit repair. Because? Because lenders charge people for so-called "subprime" higher interest rates. How much can it be? A $ 20,000 car that is funded over five years at an interest rate of 14% for anyone with a subprime loan costs an additional $ 4,722 interest. At 20% for someone with bad credit, the same car costs an additional $ 8,593. If a bad credit repair is effective and costs around $ 1,000 (it may be less, it may be greater), a person with less than perfect credit would still save nearly $ 4,000 and the person with poor credit would save around $ 7,500, Bad credit repair is a worthwhile investment.

None of this can be achieved if you are currently late with payments to lenders, be they credit cards or loans. You may need debt management or credit counselling. Still, you don't need credit repair information until you can overcome these problems. Credit counselling is useful when you are overhead, but it is not the same as a bad credit report repair. Even if you have had a bankruptcy, a bad credit report repair can be helpful.

Sometimes you can get some results on your own, but it can be time-consuming, frustrating and ineffective. Nor do you know all you can get if you don't contact a lawyer who specializes in repairing bad debt reports. Only a few options are mentioned in the credit repair information from credit bureaus and government agencies. How to report inconsistencies or inaccuracies. Sometimes the items are not removed on time, even if the credit department says no. If you can't afford to hire a law firm, you can start repairing a bad credit report by writing a letter by forwarding the information in your credit report to the appropriate credit bureau. You have 30 days to reply. The suggestions for writing these letters and addresses for the three major credit bureaus are listed in a previous post. You should try to keep all the emotions out of these letters and formulate your request in very simple words. It may be necessary to write a follow-up letter if the credit bureau does not respond in time. This letter should also be emotionless and simply state that you have waited a reasonable amount of time (30-45 days) and that you want to remove the incorrect information immediately and send a new copy of the report to your home address. If you see a company selling a so-called credit repair kit, check the contents before buying. The previous credit repair information (related to the content of the letters, etc.) is what they usually sell.

If you can get results, you are even closer to repairing bad debt reports. If the credit authority doesn't react to the subsequent letter, just a legal advisor can be reached.

CHAPTER - 1

WHAT CREDIT SCORE IS NEEDED

Credit simply means your ability to borrow. As such, your credit score is a numerical representation of the risk a lender faces if they were to lend money to you. It is based on the analysis of one's credit files/ history. Another layman's definition is that it is the difference between being denied credit and being granted credit. Well, since money is often scarce, borrowing becomes a great option for sourcing funds to do whatever you want to do. It simply enables you to do things you would otherwise not afford if you were to be paying in cash. The credit score determines how lenders perceive you when advancing credit. When your score is high, it means you are a reliable borrower so you won't need to pay more but when the score is low, the lenders treat you with caution and charge you more to advance credit to you. The cost of borrowing (interest you pay) is usually linked to your credit score. In other terms, the credit score determines how much you pay for a mortgage, health insurance, car insurance, and lots of other things including your utilities, cell phones, car payments, etc. Employers also look into credit scores lately before hiring, which means this can determine whether you are hired or not. As you may have noticed, if your score is not good, your life can be pretty much a nightmare. You will probably not even fathom the idea of living in your dream home, or driving your dream car because getting these will be literally out of your reach. Don't get me wrong, these people that run from their debts are not bad. Maybe they have a reason to stop paying off their debts. While a few missed payments may seem harmless, it does your permanent damage.

Even if you don't outright share the device with anyone, it may be that someone is actively looking for these items perhaps in an attempt to harm you. This is not to sound paranoid. There are plenty of stories where the items on someone's device have been used against them, whether by a jilted lover, private investigator, divorce attorney, co-worker, business rival, nosy neighbor, troll, hacker, or even overzealous governmental authorities.

This damage becomes apparent when you try to borrow money from lenders, or when you get a new credit card. The fact that you missed some payments is permanently reflected on your credit score.

The Purpose of Credit Scores

Credit scores are designed to mitigate various types of risk. The most commonly mentioned risk is that of lending money to a borrower. It determines one's credit worthiness i.e. how lending money to you is risky. Here is a summary of why credit scoring is great.

- Credit scores allow people to get loans faster (almost instantly) since lenders can speed up the approval process. It is possible to make instant credit decisions if you are a lender, which means this helps borrowers to access credit fast.

- It is an objective way of making credit decisions: This focuses on facts rather than feelings which are unverifiable.

- There is more credit: Lenders approve more loans based on credit.

- Lower credit rates: There are more lenders (credit), which increases competition thus pushing the cost of credit lower.

Why should your credit score be high?

- Cheaper credit: Lenders are more willing to offer a lower interest rate.

Here is a practical scenario:

- A credit score of 750 translates to a 6.11 interest on a 30-year $300,000 mortgage, while a credit score of 620 translates to a 7.42 interest on the same mortgage. As you can see, this difference will definitely translate into thousands of dollars over the 30-year mortgage period.

- It puts you on an equal footing with creditors and lenders. You can comfortably negotiate knowing that lenders are competing to have you as their good risk borrower.

- In addition, businesses develop interest in your business because it is a high value asset courtesy of the low risk.

- Insurance companies also request your credit report before deciding your premiums or even whether they will cover a risk for you.

How a Credit Score is Calculated

Your FICO score is a measure of the overall quality of your credit. While it is not the only available metric for determining credit score, it is the one that is most commonly used by a wide range of different lenders and companies when it comes to determining the level of risk that is associated with a given individual.

The calculations that go into determining a

person's credit score are proprietary which means that the Fair Isaac Company doesn't share them with anyone. However, some of the details regarding it have been found out, including the fact that a FICO score is based on a handful of different categories at various levels of importance to the total. It has been determined that payment history is weighted with approximately 35 percent relevance, the amount owed has a 30 percent relevance, credit history length has a 15 percent relevance, abundance of new credit has a 10 percent relevance and the type of credit used has a 10 percent relevance.

Payment history relates to how prompt you have been when it comes to previous payments you have made to various creditors. It also factors in things such as delinquency, number of accounts you have in collections, bankruptcy and how long it has been since these problems appeared on your record. As such, the greater number of problems you have had in this regard, the worse your overall FICO score is going to be.

When it comes to the amount you currently owe to lenders, FICO takes into account the amount of debt you currently have as well as the types of accounts you hold and the number of different accounts that you currently hold.

CHAPTER - 2

FACTORS THAT AFFECT YOUR CREDIT SCORE

The three main credit bureaus calculate your FICO score when assigning you a credit score. FICO scores are made up of the five key factors of "payment history, current level of indebtedness, types of credit used, length of credit history, and new credit accounts" (Hayes, 2019, para. 1) to calculate your score. Since the biggest companies focus on these factors, bringing up your credit score most commonly involves addressing these areas and making changes where necessary to score better in each field. While all five factors contribute to your overall score, your payment history and your current level of debt are weighted the heaviest, so let's look at these first.

Past Payment History

Your payment history is usually the most important factor in determining your credit score. It supplies information about all of your previous debt payments, including how quickly you paid them off, whether you met all payment due dates on time, if you incurred any late fees, and if you repeatedly missed payments and ended up in collections. This score is calculated using all forms of repayment, which is everything from home mortgages to credit cards to student loan debt. It does not include loans given to you by friends and family, as these loans are not reported to credit bureaus, and typically the only thing you risk by not paying them back in a timely manner is incurring your friends' wrath.

Though it is called a payment history, this does not mean that a few missteps will permanently keep you from a higher credit score. Debts that go to collections and declaring bankruptcies can impact your credit score severely when they occur, but if you proceed to build up many on-time payments and demonstrate that you have changed the way you handle your finances, it can help to balance these less positive events out and even outweigh them.

Payment history gives lenders the best picture of what you are like as a debtor and how much of a risk you would be should they approve you. This is why it accounts for such a large portion of your credit score; in fact, payment history makes up 35 percent of a FICO credit score, which is much higher than any other single factor. The best way to ensure you have a healthy credit score is to make sure your payment history is in order, which you can achieve by always making at least the minimum payments on time and trying not to use the maximum amount of credit granted to you.

Total Amount of Debt

Even if you always make your payments on time, your total debt can negatively impact your credit score. Your level of debt makes up 30 percent of a FICO credit score, making it nearly as influential as your payment history. Having too many outstanding debts can make creditors unwilling to give you a new one, as they are uncertain whether or not you can handle so much debt at a time. For example, if you already owe $80,000 in student loans, it can be hard to get approved for a mortgage on a $300,000 house, as it would saddle you with a very high amount of debt altogether. The higher your total debt, the less likely you are to be able to pay it off, which can make lenders uncertain.

Your debt burden is also impacted by your credit utilization, or the ratio of how much credit you are currently using versus how much is allowed to you. If you have a credit card with a credit limit of $4,000 and you are only using $300, this is going to reflect better than if you were using $3,000 of credit. Credit balances that are maxed out or over the available limit really hurt your score in this category.

Keep in mind that your current income level is not part of your credit score, so even if you make much more than your current debts, they can still harm your score. Say you make $150,000 a year, but you have $30,000 in unpaid credit card debt. You could probably afford to pay a great deal of it, but if you merely make the minimum payment each month, the remainder still counts as outstanding debt. If you can make payments and reduce your debts, you should do so whenever possible.

Length of Credit History

The length of your credit history is based on both the age of each line of credit on your report and how long you have been working on your credit. It makes up 15 percent of your FICO credit score, so it is relatively important, but not a game changer. This is good, because for those who have only just started to build their credit, there is not much you can do to alter this score other than simply wait it out. Younger people often have trouble with this aspect, as many do not consider credit to be a necessity until they encounter a credit roadblock that gets in the way of a purchase. This is why it is always a good idea to start looking at your credit as early as possible.

Having a longer credit history provides a pattern of behavior that showcases a more complete picture of your financial habits. Someone who has only had credit for a few months may be great at paying off their debts on time, but have more difficulty doing so as time goes on. On the other hand, a brief period of financial turmoil is more easily remedied in a longer credit history of making payments on time. This is true for both individual credit lines and your credit history as a whole.

Types of Credit

Different types of credit affect your credit score in different ways, and having a variety of credit sources rather than many of the same kind of lines of credit can help your score. Credit is broken down into three main types known as revolving credit, installment credit, and open credit. Each of these types deals with different sources of loans. Your mix of these different credit types accounts for 10 percent of your FICO credit score. While it is far from the most important factor, having a good balance of credit types can still bring your score up a few points. To do so, you must know what each category of credit means.

The first type, **revolving credit**, is commonly associated with credit cards and home equity loans. It does not require you to make a fixed number of payments, but you are required to pay a minimum balance based on how much debt you have every term, usually monthly. Revolving credit also typically charges interest on unpaid debt, and usually sets a credit limit on how much you can borrow at a time. Aside from your credit limit and monthly payments, revolving credit is relatively unstructured, and allows you to pay off your debts at your own leisure provided you continue to make at least the minimum payment.

Installment credit usually deals with larger loans that you take out for big life events. These can be student loans, auto loans, mortgages, personal loans, or many other kinds. Repayment is much more structured than with revolving credit. Payments are regularly scheduled and require a fixed amount that does not fluctuate under normal circumstances, though certain factors like changes to the terms of your loan or attempts to refinance can alter the amount you are required to pay each period. Most forms of installment credit will take a while to pay off in full, unlike revolving credit, which tends to be much more manageable to pay all at once.

Open credit is much less common than either of the above types, but can still occur, usually in the case of charge cards. The main difference between charge cards and their revolving credit counterparts, credit cards, are how much of the balance needs to be paid off each term. Generally, charge cards and any other forms of open credit require you to pay the entire balance at the end of a payment period, while credit cards usually have a minimum payment that does not account for the entire bill. Open credit typically does not have a spending limit either.

Ideally, you should have at least two different kinds of credit rather than having all your credit be the same type. However, it is not worth opening new accounts just to achieve this goal, as your credit diversity accounts for a low portion of your score and opening too many accounts can negatively impact your credit, negating any positive effects.

Amount of New Credit

This is a less well-known factor, but the number of new credit lines you open within the last year can impact your score. New credit makes up 10 percent of your FICO score, which is not a large percentage but still worth keeping in mind. Oftentimes, especially for younger people and those newer to credit, you will be tempted to open multiple different accounts to start building your credit, but opening too many in a short period can actually harm it. You should try to keep your number of new accounts to just one or two per year if you can, as this will minimize the impact on your score.

Opening new lines of credit can hurt your score because each new line of credit you apply for must check your credit score. Checking your score too frequently can negatively impact it, so too many creditors making credit inquiries can be more trouble than it is worth. Additionally, a new line of credit lowers your length of credit history, a score factor, so you will want to avoid making an unreasonable number of new accounts in a year.

CHAPTER - 3

THE IMPORTANCE OF A GOOD CREDIT SCORE

We all know how important a good credit score is, but we often don't know how to improve it. A good relationship is significant for enhancing the creditworthiness of the market. It can help you in many ways and talk about your clean background. It reflects your personality and your character. Employers also prefer someone with a good score and a clean relationship. It is synonymous with sensitivity and responsibility. If you're at a loss and don't know how to improve your score, check out our credit guide. This will help you understand the importance of a good score and suggest some ways and means of getting a desirable score.

How to Get Help?

At this point, as you read this article, you may experience the following problems.

- A poor or falling credit rating.

- Think about foreclosure or filing for bankruptcy.

- Invoices or credit card loans over the limit or pending.

- Threats for non-payment of bills, loans or mortgages.

Faced with one of these problems, you can get help from a variety of sources. These financial difficulties are common and can force you to lose your way. Several companies and agents are waiting to attract such gullible customers. They can mislead you and cause you further difficulties. You could work in your interest instead of in your interest. Several agencies of this type have unsatisfied customers who have been deceived. If you want to resolve your situation and work on the current financial situation, you need to read the relevant guide. Here are some ways you can improve your scores.

Tips to Improve Your Score

Plastic Money - The first thing you need to do to improve your score is to stop using plastic money. If you've already created a large invoice, you can order it, but no longer use the card. Reduce your purchases for a while until you are in control of the situation again.

Report - Request a report and rate the area

you need to work on. You also need to review the reports to determine if there are errors carefully. Check for incorrect information. Has it corrected by writing to the office about it?

Pay your bills on time - use your salary to pay your bills on time. Don't be late in paying. Late payment not only involves fees and expenses but is also reflected negatively in the relationship. Make sure you pay all your bills on time.

Don't fall victim to scam repair - discover the federal law that governs this system. Some people fall victim to such repair agencies. It is better to face the situation alone. If necessary, contact the State Commission for more information on the procedure. You can also read books on credit. It's important to keep the situation under control before it gets worse and makes you fail.

Why It Is So Important to Have A Good Credit Score?

The credit score is a numerical expression for the statistical analysis of credit files. In simple terms, this number will help you prove your creditworthiness. The score measures past ability to repay loans and manage previously granted loans. It is usually based on the reporting information of the credit bureau. Credit card companies and banks use credit scores to assess credit risk for their consumers. You will rely on wounds to reduce losses when it comes to bad debt. It is the outcomes that can determine who is eligible for a loan and which interest rates are most appropriate, including the credit limits that individuals receive.

Credit scores can also say a lot about your character and personality and linger forever. You will never benefit from poor results in financial situations that must occur throughout your life. You can also use numbers to evaluate employers, which makes having a good score very important. It will represent your level of responsibility and sensitivity. Here are some of the situations that make good credit important:

When buying a home: a home is a huge investment that can be very difficult to make. A home loan may be needed to make your dreams come true. With a good loan, you will meet the stringent requirements that banks, like future homeowners, will make it easier for you to get the loan.

When buying a car: vehicle loans are among the most popular. Auto loans don't seem to be home loans. It is, therefore, possible to get along with bad credit scores. However, if you have bad credit, you will end up paying very high yield loans with your auto loan. The deposit is also higher for you if you have a band score.

When starting a business: Just like buying a house or car, financial support may be needed to start a business. The credit rating depends on your eligibility for that loan. This can seriously affect your ability to access a corporate loan when it is needed.

Looking for work: Nowadays, employers also run credit checks when they want to hire new employees. It is especially common in the financial sector and government institutions. A negative score can be an obstacle to this job, so it is important to maintain good credit scores.

You will also find it very important to check your credit report. A thorough review helps to identify errors. You will likewise get numerous tips and guidance on the best way to improve your credit ratings to keep up a cleaner register before you need money or business help. There are excellent websites out there that will help you check and calculate your scores and even get a free copy of them.

Before doing any real estate business, you need to know a few things about your balance. First, a copy of all three credit reports (Trans Union, Equifax and Experian) is required, which can be easily found online in this era of computer information.

The primary concern you need to search for in your momentum reports is the point at which you have recorded antagonistic data. "Unwanted information" includes things like late payments, collections, judgments, etc. If you have negative information about your relationships and have the money to pay for them, do it immediately. The better your credit, the more business you can do. However, as mentioned above, you can do business if you have bad credit. It's easier if you don't.

The accompanying table will enable you to comprehend where your credit is found:

Credit score / rating

700 or more / excellent (A + credit)

This score indicates that in the past three years, there have been no significant delays (60 days or more) for any type of loan payment. These people can get slightly better interest rates on some types of loans.

699-660 / Very good (credit)

659-620 / Voucher (one credit)

These values do not result in significant payments (60 days or more) overdue for a mortgage loan in the past two years and only a few small delays in loan payments over the past two years. These people can quickly get "market interest rates" on all types of loans, including public loans. Bankruptcies must be resolved and resolved for four years to be classified as "good".

619-590 / Fair (credit B)

This score indicates some significant delays (60 or more days) for a mortgage loan in the past two years and widespread minor delays in loan payments over the past three years. These people receive slightly higher interest rates for all types of loans, except for public loans (FHA, VA), which are not based solely on credit scores.

589-480 / Bad (credit C)

This score indicates MANY significant delays (60 days or more) overdue for a mortgage in the past two years and widespread MAJOR payments (60-90 days) for loan payments over the past three years. People with a C loan generally receive higher interest rates and higher equity or a higher down payment for all types of loans except public loans.

In most cases, 520 is the type of approval limit for portfolio loan buyers whose loans are led by actions. Bankruptcies must be paid at the time of applying for a loan to be classified as "bad". Current amortizations, bad debts and sentences sometimes don't have to be repaid to get a mortgage. However, the penalty is a small pool of lenders, high-interest rates and stiff prepayment penalties if you refinance within three years.

Another factor in deciding your financial assessment is the number of solicitations you have. Numerous applications are dismissed because the candidate has an excessive amount of solicitations. As a general rule, "too many" requests are defined as more than 6-8 requests in your credit report. Credit bureaus have informed creditors that a person with more than this in their credit report is jumping around looking for credit, generally indicating that they are desperate or inattentive. Of course, they never think that you could simply look for the best loan.

If you have more than 6-8 requests in your credit reports, the new FCRA (Fair Credit Reporting Act) states that no requests can remain in your report for more than a year. If your report shows previous requests, you can remove duplicate requests.

It is essential to know your balance. If your score is between 620 and 700 or more, you can negotiate better conditions and interest rates on your loans. But if your credit is lower, you can still get credit, but all you have to do is "turn" and take a higher interest rate until your credit improves.

Before doing business, we cannot stress the importance of knowing your balance.

1. A borrower with a score of 680+ is considered for an A + loan. This type of loan includes the essential subscription, probably through a "computerized automated subscription" system, which is completed in a few minutes and can be completed in a few days.

2. A borrower with a score below 680 but over 620 will find that lenders take a closer look when applying for a loan. Additional credit documents and explanations may be requested before making a subscription decision. This evaluation area may allow borrowers to obtain an A loan, but it can take anywhere from a few days to several weeks to complete.

3. A borrower with a score below 620 can be excluded from the best loan rates and conditions. These borrowers are usually redirected to alternative funding sources.

Remember, just because your credit isn't A +, with patience and some creative funding, you can still do the business you want to do. Your credit can and will consistently change, and as you begin working together and reimbursing these loan specialists, it will bit by bit increment. This makes financing your offers simpler and more straightforward. Be quiet and constant and recall the significance of knowing your equalization.

CHAPTER - 4

WHAT DETERMINES YOUR CREDIT SCORE

We understand there are credit companies, credit, credit bureaus, and so on. But who does the calculation, what if it is wrong, how do they even determine your actual credit score?

What Determines Your Credit Score?

First, a credit score is a 3-digit figure that summarizes your chances of paying up a loan. It is a score generated based on particular statistics on your credit record, and you would usually get your credit score on your credit report.

Your credit score is not static. It changes according to the situation for which you have requested a credit report. As a practical example, you may request your credit report when getting into a dealership contract a get a 679 score. Then, you find 790 when you request your credit report towards a mortgage. You might say, it is situation-specific. But that is not all. It is also determined by the scoring model adopted in calculating your credit score. What does that even mean? I am about to tell you, trust me.

As FICO had proven your credit report contains four vital bits of information. Since these factors are all that make up your credit report, whatever gives your score must be something among them. Logical, right? Great. So, let's examine these factors according to their sections:

Personally, Identifiable Information (PII)

Your personal information is the first segment you will hit on your credit profile. According to FICO, your PII would include your full name, social security number, and date of birth. That is not all; your gender, location, business, and employer information are also included. You will also find a personal statement section. So that you know; your personally identifiable information is merely for the records. It is to guarantee that the credit transactions are yours, and they are not jumbled up even when there is someone who bears your exact name. You don't get a single score from this. Onto the next!

Credit History.

Okay. Here is the next phase. The credit account section is where you find the most essential details about all of your credit transactions. The details of all your credit accounts are documented here. For example, if you've got at a credit card loan with a credit union. Necessary to add, you will find details of your auto loan, mortgage, business loans, and so on in this section. But this is only IF your loan is still active and documented.

As I have shown earlier. There are chances that you could get a loan that would never reflect on your credit. It is also possible that you get a loan, and round off the payment before calling for your credit report. In that case, the loan will be reflected on your credit report. A concise breakdown of how you paid that loan will also be reflected. This means the credit report will be meticulous enough to tell any reader whether you have promptly paid the previous loan in line with the terms you agreed with the credit union OR not. That may not be good news, so you have got to take the rule of every loan earnestly.

Another thing, all of your credit transactions can't reflect on your credit report. The first type of such are off-the-table transactions that I have told you about; your transaction with friends, unregistered companies, and private credit transactions in general. You need to know that credit companies often require a credit report. They are always interested in other loans you

have taken at some point. So, if you have taken no loan earlier and you are looking forward to one, it makes perfect sense to start with a credit card. Draw credits even when you don't need them, but make them minimal and clear them as soon as you can. It gives banks a sense of warmth and assurance. You paid back early because you hate owing. You also drew a loan because you are not an alien to loans, even when you don't need so much of it.

That is out. The next set of loans that may not reflect on your credit report are withdrawn debts. Withdrawn debts are debts that have been found irrelevant, wrong, and in some way, unworthy to be fitted to your records. So, it gets skimmed out. For example, you have just received a claim that you took some credit from Sam Credit Union. If you refute it and the company can't prove that you have some existing loans with them, that record gets scrapped. Even in cases when you took that loan in reality, and you are sure that your creditor or credit union does not have ample information to back that loan, that record will be shucked off when you call for that.

In previous cases, many business people took a loan from their friends and made it reflect on their credit report. Their friends may tick that loan as paid, so it gives a positive impression in the credit records, even when it is just make-believe. They find some way to settle the debts of the records. That sounds like a trick to boost a positive impression on your profile. But it's not always so. According to a business magazine, many of such cases got to court because the businessman refused to pay that debt, assuming his friend has got no proofs. Again, these friends may get into a dispute over some other issues and decide to expose each other. Even couples went down in the dumps and exposed each other. So, this may not be a great idea.

Drawing this to a close, I should tell you that bad credit and public records can also be removed from your records. If you have declared bankruptcy, had horrible court decisions on your credit, and so on, they are removed from your credit report after some time. Once this time lapses, you can hold out for their removal and wipe them off your credit records permanently.

Credit Inquiries

Next is Credit Inquiries. As Latoya Irby, a credit analyst, chooses to put it; Credit Inquiries is a general term that covers all investigations and requests for your credit report. As you now understand, credit companies want you to have a credit report before accessing their services; as such, you are bound to create a credit report before you get real loans. But the credit companies don't just want you to set the records. They want to explore it.

Practically, this means that each time you call for loans in a credit company, you are bound to permit them to request for your credit report from a credit bureau. They usually do, and the detail of each inquiry is inserted in the next credit report. For example, if A/B Company had requested your report at some point, and KYC Company had also requested, JJC Company will find these companies in your credit report when you apply for another credit with them. That way, they can tell the other people you have contacted, how 'desperate' you have been finding some credit, and how un/successful you have been. That may not be an impressive spotlight.

Public Records

Lastly, but equally important. Your public records will be found in your credit report. Just the same way your pertinent personal information is displayed, relevant public records are shown on your credit report.

As a practical example, if you have had a dispute and court cases on a credit transaction, it will be shown here. In the case that you have declared bankruptcy, foreclosure, et cetera, these situations will also be displayed at this section of your credit report.

Depending on what you have got here, this may be a plus or a curse to your loan application. But it doesn't matter so much. This is one of the records that can be evicted from your records at some point. Some records take seven years; some take ten before you can get them off. Yet, they will be off at some point. So, if you got some depressing ones already, keep your cheeks alive.

Now, we have extensively worked over the elements in your credit report. We can talk about which of them determines your credit score. Shall we? Great!

As we have earlier identified, credit scores are determined by Credit Scoring Models. What are those?

Credit Scoring Models

These are specialized agencies that develop scoring formats for credit bureaus. According to the Federal Statistics, there are over 50 of them in the United States. Of that, only FICO, a model designed by Fair Isaac Company, is widely used and accepted everywhere. It is often adopted by the three most popular credit bureaus in the country too. Fairly, FICO is trailed by Vantage, Community Empower, TransUnion, Xpert, Insurance, and some others.

Due to this diversity, it is impossible to generate

an all-purpose method of calculating credit scores. So, it would be impossible to tell how each company measures your credit performance concisely. It is clear however, these scoring models usually generate 3-digit as your credit score, which means you may rank anywhere between 300- 850 (or 950).

CHAPTER - 5

THE BENEFITS OF GOOD CREDIT

A person with a bad credit score can still obtain credit but may feel the consequences are too much. A poor credit score will result in high-interest rates that can quickly become expensive, especially if you take longer to pay your accounts. A good, excellent, or exceptional credit score will reduce the interest charges and help you to save money in the long run. There are many other benefits to having a good credit score.

Lower Interest Rates

Any person who has credit will need to pay interest on the outstanding account balance. The amount you borrow is often referred to as the capital balance. The balance outstanding is equal to the interest charges and the capital balance together. You can see interest as the profit the lending company gets for giving you credit; some places call it a financing cost. It is a fee that is levied every month in proportion to the amount of credit you have used and not yet paid back. A poor credit score will result in a higher interest rate and thus having to pay more fees. The advantage of a good credit score is a lower interest rate and pay fewer fees.

The lower interest cost makes it easier to pay back your capital balance. Most people are only paying back interest and then have the interest charged again on a monthly basis, which results in a vicious circle of only paying the interest. If you are only paying interest then it is difficult to pay back the capital balance you have borrowed. The better credit score and result in a lower interest rate can work to your advantage. It makes it possible to pay both interest and capital balance and, in that way, reduce your total debt.

Negotiating Possibilities

A high credit score provides leverage for negotiation. Your bank may have offered you a credit card with a set interest rate. You can approach other financial institutions and find out if they can give you a more favorable interest rate. This negotiating power helps you to find the best possible interest rate and offers with the lowest costs.

Having assets in your name will give you even more negotiating power. Lenders will always choose a customer who has security when it comes to providing credit facilities. Owning an apartment, vehicle, or other assets will give banks the knowledge that you can pay them back. Stable assets help in negotiations with financial institutions for decreasing interest rates and down payments. You should be proud of your high credit score and can always use it as leverage. Many people are scared to negotiate, but it can save you a bucket load of money in the long run. For example, an interest rate that is just 1% lower than the original quoted rate can reduce your total repayment with thousands of dollars. This money could be used in so many other ways than paying off a mortgage.

Improved Chance of Credit Approval

A better credit score makes it easier to be approved for further credit in the future. Every time you apply for credit, the financial institution will do a credit check. Your credit score is then made available to the company that made the request. The credit score will be used to help make a decision on whether the account should be opened, a credit card is issued, or a loan application approved.

Most people with a high credit score will qualify for a home loan or already have a home loan. Ensuring you make frequent payments on your mortgage can greatly contribute to a higher credit score, which will bring additional benefits. If you ever get to a point where you want to do renovations or need additional money, you can visit your home loan company and ask to refinance your home. This means that you will have funds made available to you but your mortgage will increase. You can still negotiate for good interest rates and lower fees. Plus, your long-standing relationship with the lender makes it easier to approach them for additional financing.

Great Credit Card Offers

Financial institutions want to work with customers who pay their bills every month. Your credit score is one of the things that is appealing to banks. Many banks will pull credit score information to find potential clients. The bank will then contact you and offer you some great credit card deals. Your own bank is also likely to provide you with better credit terms. If you get a call from a financial institution offering to provide you with a beneficial credit card, then you are most likely doing a great job with keeping your credit score high. Listen to the offer and ask the contact person to send you more information via email. You can then check the options and decide if this credit card is a good idea.

A solid credit score will lead to offers of credit cards with good rewards and other benefits.

Some lenders will provide a credit card account to you without charging any monthly fees. Other institutions have rewards programs linked to the credit card. Using your credit card responsibly and for certain transactions will give you points or a specific reward's level. A higher score will qualify you for more rewards. The rewards can include reduced prices on air-plane tickets or discounted rates on accommodation. Some financial institutions will add extra insurance cover, roadside assistance, or a personal banker to take your calls at any time of the day.

Better Insurance Rates

Car insurance is very important to protect you in the case of an accident, whether it is your fault or not. Automotive insurers look closely at credit scores when determining insurance premiums. The same goes for home owner's insurance. You need to have insurance to cover costs should your property ever sustain any damage. A person with a low credit score is perceived to be a high-risk client. The insurance company assumes that these people are more likely to claim from the insurance for unnecessary or fraudulent claims. This lack of trust results in higher insurance premiums.

A similar concept to the credit score is an

insurance score used in some companies. The scores are not exactly the same but the general principle of a higher score is better stays the same. Your credit score will greatly influence your insurance score. People with a high credit score are seen as more trustworthy by the insurance companies. They benefit from lower insurance premiums thanks to a good credit record. Additionally, insurance claims may be paid more easily if you are in an accident or have damage to your home. After a claim, your insurance provider may increase the monthly premium to help cover some additional costs and to decrease risk. A higher credit score can be used to help negotiate a lower premium. Always ask your insurance provider to take your credit record into consideration when calculating your monthly premiums and excess amounts.

Better Rental Agreements

Landlords who rent out the property are always concerned about receiving their rental income. Many times, a landlord will advertise an apartment but they don't know the people who eventually rent from them. Your credit score is one way for the landlord to learn more about prospective tenants. The landlord or rental agency will often use your credit report to see if you pay on time or miss payments. Often times, landlords are more willing to let property to people with a high credit score and will out rightly reject applicants with a low credit score. A person with a good credit score is more likely to be approved for renting property since the landlord knows that the person is likely to pay.

Landlords are more open to working with people who have a high credit score, which makes the rental relationship much easier. For example, a person with a high credit score may be able to negotiate for a lower security deposit, or even have the possibility of paying the security deposit over a two-month period rather than paying the full amount at once. On the flip side, a person with a low credit score will most likely be asked to pay a substantially higher security deposit.

Fewer Security Deposits

A security deposit is often requested by companies as it shows that you will pay your account in the future. If you do not make payments, then the credit provider can use the security deposit to recover some of the costs. Security deposits are used by companies that provide both products and services.

Cellphone companies often require a security deposit since the customer gets the phone before full payment has been received by the company. This situation is very risky for cellphone providers. The security deposit can cover some of the costs if a person stops paying their cellphone account. Other companies that may require a security deposit are those which offer utilities, such as gas and water. A person with a high credit score often has the benefit of not paying a security deposit or paying significantly less. Your credit history and credit score have proven that you pay your bills on time and provides peace of mind for the company.

Self-Confidence

One of the biggest benefits of a good credit score is the boost your self-confidence experiences. You should be proud of yourself for saving your money and using your credit wisely. A good credit score takes time and effort to achieve. Achieving a high rating deserves a pat on the back. You also know that you can easily use your finances responsibly in the future.

CHAPTER - 6

BASICS OF CREDIT REPAIR

By making your financial goals, setting your budget, finding ways to save money, and requesting a copy of your credit report, you've done your preliminary legwork in trying to get your finances back in order.

Now that all three credit reporting agencies have a copy of your credit report, it's time to roll up your sleeves and tackle the inaccurate information reported on your credit report.

Reviewing Your Credit Report

When you check each of your credit reports, whether it is on the website of the credit reporting agency where you can download it, or a hard copy of your report which you received in the mail, it is vital that each entry is accurately reported.

When you consider misleading or incorrect information on the credit report, the Equal

Credit Reporting Act notes you have the right to dispute the submission with the credit reporting agency. The credit reporting agency has to re-examine the creditor's admission. The enquiry must be concluded within 30 days of receiving the lawsuit message.

If the borrower fails to respond within that time period, the credit reporting agency must delete from the credit report the entry you are contesting. If the creditor replies and the inaccurate entry is corrected, the credit reporting agency will update your credit report. There is also the risk that the borrower can respond to the credit report and not make any changes in it. If you're not happy with your revised credit report, you should write a 100-word paragraph to clarify your side of the story on any of the remaining items on the credit report. This customer statement will then surface any time it appears on your credit report. If you don't want to write a 100-word paragraph on your credit report, you will be able to write another 120-day appeal letter from your most recent credit report.

The Disputing Process

The first thing you need to know is that all three credit reporting agencies have to contest the inaccurate information independently. The disputed appearance may be on all three credit reports, or may not. Keep in mind that customers may not belong to all credit reporting agencies. This is why you will see that on one list some of the investors are not on the others.

Even though all three credit reporting agencies have the same information, this does not mean that if an item comes out of one credit report it will come out of the others. No promise is provided what the outcome will be. That is why you have to refute any inaccurate information about each particular article.

When you access your credit report on the Website of the credit reporting agency, you will be able to dispute the incorrect entries online. The site will have boxes to check for inaccuracy alongside an appropriate reason. If you choose to write a personalized message, you can also use the same answers as appropriate. Sample answers would be:

- This is not my account.

- This was not late as indicated.

- This was not charged off.

- This was paid off in full as agreed.

- This was not a collection account.

- This is not my bankruptcy as indicated.

- This is not my tax lien as indicated.

- This is not my judgment as indicated.

If you've found more than four entries on your credit report that you need to dispute, don't dispute everything in one letter. Whether you're writing a letter, filling out their form or answering via the Internet, break your disputes. You send or go back every 30 days to the website of the credit reporting agency, and challenge up to four more things. Don't overshoot that number. If you have to challenge less than four things, go ahead and dispute the remaining entries. Extend the spacing of conflicts for 30 days.

On submitting each address, expect to receive a revised credit report about 45 days after you send your letter or disagreement online. If your new credit report has not been issued before it's time to appeal the second time, go ahead and mail your second letter or challenge online instead.

Once all the grievance letters have been mailed or posted to their website and all the revised credit reports have been received, check whether products have been omitted or incomplete. If you need to do the procedure again for the remaining items, space 120 days from your most recent update to the next round of disputes.

What You Shouldn't Do:

- Alter your identity, or try to change it.

- The story is fictional.

- Check any information which is 100% correct.

What You Should Do:

- Read your emails, should you decide to send them to us. If a letter looks legitimate, credit reporting agencies will believe it has been written by a credit repair service, and they will not investigate the dispute.

- Use your original letterhead (if you do have one).

- Use the appeal form included with the credit report by the credit reporting agency, if you want.

- Provide some evidence suggesting the wrong entry is erroneous.

- Include the identification number for all communications listed on the credit report.

Common Credit Report Errors

Note, there could be various mistakes in each of the three credit reports. It is not uncommon to have positive coverage of an account on one article, but poor reports on another.

Here are some of the most common credit report errors.

- Listed wrong names, emails, or phone

numbers.

- Data that refers to another of the same name.

- Duplicate details, whether positive or negative, about the same account.

- Records have negative, apparently positive information.

- Balances on accounts payable are still on view.

- Delinquent payment reports that were never billed in due time.

- This indicates wrong credit limits.

- Claims included in the insolvency which are still due.

- Incorrect activity dates;

- Past-due payments not payable.

- Court records which are falsely connected with you, such as convictions and bankruptcy.

- Tax liens not yours.

- Unprecedented foreclosures.

Spotting Possible Identity Theft

Checking your credit report could also spot potential identity theft. That's why you should inquire at least once a year or every six months for a copy of your credit report.

Things to look for would be:

- Names of accounts and figures that you do not know.

- You don't remember filling out loan applications.

- Addresses you didn't live in.

- Poor bosses or tenants' enquiries you don't know.

Creditors Can Help

Many times, if you have had a long-term account with a creditor, you can contact them directly and explain the error being reported on your credit report.

Ask them to write you a letter with the email and correction. Also ask them to contact every credit reporting agency that reports this incorrect entry in order to make the correction.

Once the creditor receives a copy of the letter, make a copy of it and attach the letter to the letter of dispute you send. Mail it to the agency for credit reporting, and ask them to update their files. Once that is completed, you will be sent back a new credit report by the credit reporting agency.

Credit Rescoring

Rapid rescoring is an expedited way of fixing anomalies in the credit file of a customer. The bad news is, you can't do it yourself. A fast rescore dispute process works through borrowers and mortgage brokers, a number of approved registry credit reporting companies, and credit reporting agencies.

If you are a creditor applying for a rescore on your credit report, you would need to provide detailed documents that would be sent to the collateral agencies that are working on your case. Cash registry is the system used by cash grantors. The data archive gathers the records from the three main credit reporting agencies, and has to check the consumer's initial information for a rescore. Once the verification is entered into the program of the repository a new score will be produced.

The key thing to keep in mind is that a simple rescore can only be temporary. You may be able to close a loan with it, but you must follow through on your credit report with the three main credit reporting firms to ensure it has been removed or corrected. If it reappears, forward the reports immediately to credit reporting agencies.

The downside of a fast rescore is that you save money without having to contend individually with a credit reporting agency that may take longer than 30 days to complete an audit. If the sale of a house or lease depends on your credit score, and you're in a time crunch, the best solution is to rescore easily.

Should You Use a Credit Repair Company?

Using a credit repair company's services is basically hiring a firm to do what you can do for yourself. The process is really without secrets. All the credit repair company does is dispute information on negative entries on your credit report with credit reporting agencies. Most companies may report having agreements with credit reporting agencies or have a secret way to get borrowers to delete unfavorable entries. This is more than likely not true because the credit reporting agencies are regulated by both state and federal laws under the Fair Credit Reporting Act.

The reason some people hire an outsourced credit repair company is because they feel intimidated or have no time to do the work themselves. Until signing up with a credit repair company there are many steps you need to take. Many businesses operate illegally and you don't want to get caught in that trap.

Beware of Credit Repair Scams

Sadly, it is easy for people to fall prey to credit

repair fraud when they are vulnerable and are going through financial challenges. If you're looking for a repair company for cash, here's how to say if it's a genuine or scam business. Many scam firms may only sign up to take the money and run for their services. This is a list of stuff that should raise a red flag.

- The company doesn't tell you your rights, and you can do it for free. This should appear in any document it presents you with.

- The firm advises that you do not explicitly approach any of the three major national credit reporting agencies. It knows that if you do, you may learn that it took your money, and that it does nothing.

- The company tells you that even if that information is accurate, it can get rid of all the negative credit reports in your credit report. No one can promise just one thing on your credit report for change.

- The company assumes you're trying to create a "different" credit identifier. This is known as file segregation. It is accomplished by filing for the use of an Employer Identification Number to create a new credit report instead of the Social Security number. That is utterly unconstitutional.

- The firm encourages you to challenge any

information contained in your credit report regardless of accuracy or timeliness of the material. If the evidence is 100% right, then you have no basis for a disagreement. s

Remember, if you are given unlawful advice and follow it knowing it is illegal, you may be committing fraud, and you will find yourself in lawful hot water.

CHAPTER - 7

STARTING FROM THE SCRATCH AND MAINTAINING IT

How to Build Credit Score Quickly?

It is nothing but the "score" you accumulate over time and which defines you as a good or bad debtor. I'll explain. If you have a loan of any kind, the more you pay on time and the more your Credit Score goes up if instead, you accumulate delays or unpaid installments your Credit Score drops one round of hell at a time (I think Dante's Inferno he referred to this when he wrote it!)

It is important that you take care of your score consistently because over time it will be the first thing that banks, or loan companies, will see when you ask for a loan to buy a house, a car or anything else. At the moment, it may not seem important but trust me, you will change your mind. I've been there. I didn't give enough importance to it, and when it was time, I regretted it.

The credit card is not the prerogative of Dad's children (except for some cases), but something that young people use to start building their Credit Score from an adolescent age. Unfortunately, we are not 16 years old so we must try to catch up as soon as possible. The problem with the Credit Score is that it is difficult to build when you have no loans or credit cards and it is almost impossible to get either of these if you do not have a Credit Score. In practice, a cat that bites its tail.

How to build a Credit Score from scratch?

There are several ways and all of them are effective.

1.   The first is to open a bank account. Having an account open in itself will not increase your score, but it will give you a starting point to show regular income. After a few months, you can ask your bank (remember to show off your best smile) what services they offer to increase your Credit Score. My bank, for example, offers a mini-loan of $ 500 tied up to be returned in 6 months. It means that you deposit $ 500, they re-loan them to you at a favorable rate and when, in 6 months, you finish paying the installments, they give you back the $ 500 in the barrel. Practically in 6 months, you paid interest as a "tax" with the sole purpose of accumulating points. To put it in simpler words:

from 500 and 500 you return, then you pay 500 in installments + interest and you return 500 at the end. It is an expense, but this type of loan guarantees you a considerable accumulation of points, but only if you are regular in payments.

2.   The second, and in my opinion the best, is to apply for a Secured Credit Card. Unlike traditional credit cards, you do not have to show any kind of entry to get approval, but you also have a usage limit. The only thing required is a deposit which is returned to you after a year of regular use. Until a couple of years ago, the deposit was around 200 euros, but with the debt problems that developed after the recession, all the major credit companies have lowered the costs. For example, I applied with Capital One (but there are many others like Discover). The deposit was only $ 49 and the card limit was $ 200 a month with the option of 2% cash back on gas or restaurant expenses. I started using it regularly every month ONLY for these two things and, after a year, my Credit Score was already considered very good, they also returned the deposit and the cash back and the credit limit rose to 500 dollars after only six months. We clarify that you are not obliged to use it only for these things, but I have limited myself for two reasons. The first is to accumulate cash back (i.e. a refund) at the end of the year. The second is to make sure I never use more than 30% of the

card limit. Which brings me to the next point.

3.   Never exceed 30% of the credit card limit. Believe it or not, it is essential that you show that you do not need a credit card to pay for your things, but that you use it only when strictly necessary or as an accurate choice. The more you use it constantly the better, but judiciously.

4. Pay your installments regularly. All the above points have absolutely no value if you are not constant in payments. No one here scales your loan or credit card debts from your salary. It is your responsibility to remember when you have to pay or set up an automatic payment from your bank account. I decided to set up automatic payments. As long as he has a good memory, you never know what can happen that can put you off your mind on the expiry day. So, I strongly suggest you do the same because even a missed payment will negatively affect your score.

5.   Vary the types of debt as much as you can. If you can make the Secured Card And the mini-loan with the bank at the same time, do it. The more options you have, the faster your Credit Score will grow. Of course, always keep in mind that if you don't pay on time, they show up at home with the Pit bulls (so to speak or almost). So, if you're not sure you can do better, don't risk it and wait a little longer.

6.   Add your name to someone else's credit card as an "authorized user". If, for example, if you are married to an American who has had much more time than you to accumulate a decent score (as in my case), it might be a good idea for him to indicate you as an authorized user of his credit cards. This does not mean that you will actually have to use his credit cards, but the more his score improves, the more he will positively influence yours. Be careful though! If you go down, he comes down with you. This type of choice involves a fat, large demonstration of trust so be careful not to betray it. If you mess up the Credit Score that has been sweating so much since he was in swaddling clothes, well I wouldn't want to be in your shoes!

7. Check your Credit Score regularly to make sure there are no problems you are unaware of and have such nasty surprises. Even a late paid bill can affect your payer profile. Now pay attention to the following because it's important. There are several ways to check where you are with the economic 'pregnancy'. The first is to apply here for your Annual Credit Report, but you are entitled to a free check only once a year. The second is to check directly in Credit Bureaus such as Transunion, Equifax or Experian. Also, in these cases, you can have a free check per year, or pay a monthly installment to keep your score constantly under control. Obviously, the

annual checks have their advantages, but be careful not to take too much advantage of their services. Believe it or not, every time you request a check this will lower your Credit Score. Crazy, right? And this brings me to the only sensible solution that remains to keep the score under control.

8.   Download the free Credit Karma app. Not only does it constantly give you a detailed report of your score, but also what has positively or negatively influenced, which credit cards or loans are best suited to your situation, your progress, and many other functions. It's all free and, although not updated to the minute, rather accurate. It does not lower your Credit Score and also offers you many other services such as online and free tax returns. Due to Credit Karma, other major credit companies have also had to adjust to offer the Credit Score free check. For example, Capital One and Discover have now integrated this service into their offers (although in a more limited way being a cost to them).

If you follow these tips in a year you can afford to ask for a car loan without having to pay disproportionate interest or even more, depending on your income and your general receivables/payables situation. This reminds me of how important it is to start as soon as possible.

Remember that this is the first thing they look at when you need to apply for a loan!

Credit Repair: How to Improve Your Credit Score After Foreclose or Bankruptcy

Regardless of what happened to you financially - if you have gone through foreclosure or bankruptcy, got behind on credit card payments or collected a lot of debt - you can rebuild your credit. Here's how:

Check the credit report

It is determined by a series of factors that can be divided into the following categories: credit history - How long have you been using credit?

How to Apply to For Lines of Credit

You may now have high fico scores, but that is only the beginning. At this point it is all about knowing what to do and where to go actually to turn your credit scores into leveraged money. So now that you have the scores that are needed, where do you go to get the money? If you just want to build your credit up slowly and you are not worried about having access to high credit limits, you can opt-back-in for pre-screened credit offers and apply blindly for whatever offers that may come in the mail, or you can be proactive and come up with a plan.

Going with the flow works perfectly fine for

people who are not as concerned or don't take a hands-on approach to building their credit, you will stumble across some quality credit products because these offers will be sent your way, but pre-approvals don't mean you have all the necessary requirements to obtain the actual approval, and I want to save you time by getting you started in the right direction. You might have a few ideas of where you want to apply, but is it the most effective course of action? Have you developed a funding strategy yet? I have no doubt that you will receive offers for 0% balance transfers and a lot of other incentives from companies like Citi Bank, American Express, Discover and a bunch of others, some you will actually get approved for, others will waste your time and deny you. The strategy I am going to show you will allow you to take matters into your own hands and go after what you want as far as credit limits, credit cards with benefits and accounts that will assure you maximum future growth. You want to stay away from any credit cards that will not benefit you down the road because either they lack any substantial reward incentives or room for you to grow the credit limits. You don't want to obtain high credit limits from some, just to be held down by $500 starter credit cards from others just because you were too anxious and excited to get any approval.

CHAPTER - 8

WHAT IS A FICO SCORE?

Understanding the Fico Credit Scoring Algorithm

The small company created in 1956, FICO, would change in just two years the way in which banks granted credit to the average American.

In the United States, in 1956, the engineer William Fair and the mathematician Earl Isaac met while working at Stanford Research Institute. Soon after, they launched the company Fair, Isaac and Company, which would later become FICO.

The FICO credit score is a score of 300 to 850 that assesses the level of risk the applicant has when it comes to returning a loan. Before its creation, financial institutions had little information and internally assessed whether or not they granted credit to the applicant.

This method focuses on the analysis of data

in general and on credit rating services in particular. They sold their first credit scoring system two years after the birth of the company. The FICO system was well received. He launched his system to 50 American lenders. This method of scoring, FICO, understood as a measure of consumer credit risk has now become a complement to consumer loans in the United States.

How does FICO work?

The information on which this system is based is objective and consistent. By law, creditworthiness cannot be based on the applicant's race, religion, sex or nationality. Therefore, it is a non-discriminatory system.

The points to be evaluated are three, one for each of the three risk centers: Experian, TransUnion, and Equifax. According to MyFico, the scores are based on the information that the credit bureau has about a person. If this information changes, the credit scores also change. In addition, the three scores on which they are based also affect loan conditions that loan institutions will offer us. So, what happens if we improve our scores? Well, we will have better interest rates from the institutions. It is important to be clear that new debts will have a negative impact on our score. According to Lawyers Title, the search for new credit and the opening of new credit accounts to pay previous accounts will also affect the score.

It is necessary that the three credit reports have, at least, an updated account in a minimum of six months, each one. This ensures that there is enough updated information to calculate the FICO score. There is a relationship between the risk of return and the scores: the higher the score, the lower the risk. Each lending institution has the right to choose the level of risk it is willing to accept for each loan.

Most of the scores of risk centers used in the United States are called FICO, as they are created by software developed by Fair Isaac and Company.

How "FICO 08" Impacts Your Credit Score

Delinquencies - The second change in the scoring model has to do with payment patterns - especially those that are greater than 90 days late in making a payment.

myFICO Review:

Recently I was able to spend a good deal of time visiting the myFICO website. Here you can get the most updated FICO score for only $ 19.95. But the site offers much more than your score. They have several other "tabs" on their home page that provide everything from a variety of monitoring and FICO score protection products to the latest low-interest credit cards.

FICO score defined

First, let's define what we're talking about. In today's "credit-focused" world, all the different scores and reports can be confusing. The FICO score is determined by the Fair Isaac Corporation (hence the FICO name) and is a way to measure a person's creditworthiness. It's a score that can range from 350 to 850.

This number is used to determine everything from mortgage rates to credit card terms to car loan interest rates and is used by around 90% of banks in this country.

How Credit Queries Affect Your Credit Score

Have you noticed any queries on your credit report? Not sure what they mean? Soft and hard investigations are the result of potential creditors who evaluate your credit report after requesting something like a credit card, a mortgage or a car loan. Hard and soft investigations each affect your credit differently.

"Soft" inquiries about your credit report

Do not worry. Soft inquiries do not affect your credit score. Normally, soft inquiries occur when your credit report is requested for a background check. This can happen when you are applying for a new job, get pre-approved for loan offers, and even when you verify your own credit score.

While they usually show up on your credit report, this is not always the case. Also, they will not affect your credit score, so you do not need to worry about them.

What Does This Mean to You?

There are certain cases that can result in a mild or difficult investigation depending on the situation (for example, when you rent a car or sign up for a new cable or Internet service). If you are not sure if your actions will lead to a mild or difficult investigation, you can simply ask the financial institution that is requesting funding.

Another exception is when you are making rate purchases. Generally, your FICO score will record only one investigation within a period of 14-45 days if you are shopping for the best mortgage, auto loan, or student loan rates. By making all your purchases for the same type of loan within a two-week period, you can reduce the effect on your credit.

As is the case with anything that negatively affects your credit score, investigations can affect your ability to obtain good loan rates.

The good news about a difficult investigation is that if you are not doing it often, it will not have a big effect on your credit. For example, factors such as your payment history, credit history, and credit rate are weighted much more.

CHAPTER - 9

IMPROVING THE SCORE, STEP BY STEP PLANS

Step 1: Get your credit report. Everything starts with getting your credit report and your credit score.

Step 2: Review your report for inaccurate or negative information.

Inaccurate or negative information can be harmful to your credit score. Creditors see this information and may deny you credit because of it. Not only that, but it can negatively affect your credit score, and it even may be a sign of fraudulent activity. Inaccurate information can be removed fairly easily, and if you have accurate negative information, you need to know so you can limit its impact.

The reports vary slightly depending on the credit bureau, but in general your report will have six sections:

- Personal Information

- Summary

- Account History

- Public Information

- Inquiries

- Creditor Contacts

Step 2a: Review the Personal Information Section. While this section does not directly impact your credit score, it is still a good idea to make sure the information is accurate. We have seen credit reports where personal information was confused with relatives, or other people with the same name. This confusion may lead to other mistakes which can impact your credit standing. Sometimes this information is added manually and mistakes happen, assumptions are made, and eventually creditors end up with conflicting information which is not in your interest.

Correct any information that is incorrect.

Name: If your name appears incorrectly, contact the creditor that provided the incorrect name. If you do not correct it, creditors will continue reporting the wrong name. Why is this bad? Because you are on the road to improving your credit and the wrong name may carry other misinformation that continues to weigh down your credit status. The contact information for all creditors is on the report. If you have a hyphenated name, the report may not show the hyphen.

Date of Birth: If your date of birth is wrong on the report, you should contact the credit bureau directly to change it. You will need to send the request via mail along with a copy of your driver's license and birth certificate, or state I.D.

Managing the Amounts Owed

Always try to make at least the minimum payment on your credit cards and make them on time and never miss consecutive payments. This is the magic bullet of building great credit. Having a track record of making many payments on time is golden to creditors, loan agents and the credit bureaus.

However, missing just one payment will set you back and missing multiple payments could set you back years. In fact, a single late payment can drop your credit score anywhere from 75-100 points. The creditors will believe that you have no intention of paying them once you start missing multiple payments and they will take actions that could take a very long time to repair.

Bottom line is to make at least the minimum payment a top priority, and if you can't do so, then contact the creditor as soon as possible. Explain the situation and tell them that you sincerely want to work with them. Try to set up a payment arrangement with them that will not adversely affect your credit. Some creditors may be willing to work with you and offer lower payments or additional time to pay. I recommend that you also try to find out how they will report the new arrangement to the credit bureaus, and get their answer in writing. This may or may not end up showing on your credit report, depending on how the creditor reports it, but either way, it is much better than a missed payment.

- Don't assume anything is harmless. City parking fines, library fines, cell phone bills, electricity bills and many other outstanding bills that seem insignificant can end up going to a collector when they go unpaid. Then they end up as negative items in your credit file. Simple things like these can set you back, so be diligent and keep all accounts up to date. When you change providers such as switching from a cable company to a satellite TV company, make sure your old account is paid up, and that the account actually closed. Open accounts with an unpaid balance will often turn into a delinquency and eventually end up on your credit report. Remember, we live in a computer world. Often a real person never even looks at your account which means a computer will decide if your five cent balance should be reported to the credit bureaus. Usually it is completely automated, so assume nothing!

Making payments and not closing accounts with an open debt will prevent a delinquency mark showing on your credit report. It is one of the easiest ways to keep your credit from taking a hit.

Managing Your Payment History

Damaging information can stay on your credit report for 7-10 years. Even a closed account can show negative information for up to 7 years if there was an unpaid balance when the account was closed. On the other hand, a good payment history will also counteract the negative information. For instance, a paid-in-full closed account will remain on your credit record for 7 years as well.

Managing New Credit

When you apply for credit such as with a credit card or for a loan, the creditor will make an inquiry into your credit report. One thing they will look at is how much recent activity you have had so do not initiate too much credit activity in a short period of time. By that, we mean do not apply for multiple credit cards at the same time, be careful about putting in too many applications for bank loans around the same time. Each time you do so, it creates a hard inquiry record and while credit bureaus know that everyone will apply for credit from time to time, too many inquiries may cause them to penalize your score out of fear that you are in financial trouble, or that you are about to overextend yourself by taking on multiple loans.

Other types of actions that could cause inquiries include asking for extended credit or a higher limit, or even renting a car. These are called hard inquiries and stay on your record for two years so there is not a quick fix once you land them. The possible exception is applying for a few of the same type of loans, such as a home loan, or a car loan within a 30-day period. The credit reporting agencies may count all the inquiries as only one inquiry if your credit rating is decent and it seems consistent with you just shopping around for the best rates.

Also, when you do receive new credit, make sure you make the payments on time since they weigh new credit payments heavily into the credit score.

Create A Spending Plan To Eliminate Debt

Find money to pay off debt! Paying off old debts and reducing balances needs to be a priority if it is weighing you down and damaging your credit record. Until that happens, you may find yourself constantly treading water with your credit. But what if you don't have the money? The first thing we recommend is that you set up a plan of action. Set up a monthly budget and stick to it. Any extra money left over each month goes to paying off the debt. Where possible pay off the balances that have the highest interest rate first. This will help limit the total amount owed from growing and save you money in the long run.

If you are the type of person who just can't help using a credit card, and it is creating new debt, then cancel the card. Normally we would not recommend this, since having a high credit limit helps your overall credit score. However, it is worse for you to accumulate unpaid credit card debt than to have the benefit of a higher credit limit.

Pay your taxes - Uncle Sam can really get tough when taxes go unpaid. They may foreclose, attach a lien, garnish your wages and do a lot of other things that will damage your credit, not to mention tacking on penalties and interest, virtually making it impossible to pay back. They also have special laws allowing their collections and tax liens to stay on your credit report indefinitely, even after full payment. These actions can have a negative snowball effect on your credit. If you can't pay your taxes, contact the IRS and set up a payment plan. It may keep them from taking further action against you that will damage your credit.

Monitor Your Credit – checking your credit status frequently can help you fix problems before creditors see them. It enables you to know if you will be able to negotiate the best loan rates, and should questions arise about your credit status, you will already be aware of any issues ahead of time. Also, it will alert you to possible fraud or identity theft.

If you have requested changes or opened a dispute then follow up on the changes requested. Don't assume they have been fixed. I recommend that you review all three major credit reports (Experian, TransUnion, and Equifax) every 6 months. If you are planning a significant purchase, then you should try to check your credit report about three months before the planned purchase date. This will give you time to remove or change incorrect or harmful items on the report. All three bureaus also offer credit monitoring services as well for an extra fee. Another bonus is that sometimes, by being a member of the credit monitoring services, it is a little easier to dispute inaccuracies online.

Step-By-Step Simple Plan Summary

1. Get your credit report and credit score.

2. Correct any wrong information in your credit report.

3. Do whatever it takes to pay all bills before they are due. If necessary, put them on a calendar, write yourself sticky notes, use online bill paying, set up email reminders, or make a habit to pay them the day they come in. If you can't pay, then pay the minimum or contact the creditor and let them know.

4. If you have debt weighing you down, make it a priority to pay it down. Always make the minimum payment but whenever possible, pay more. If necessary, create a spending plan and stick to it.

5. Do not apply for too much credit in a short time span.

6. If you have credit, don't run up bills that you can't afford to pay off within the next billing cycle.

7. When closing accounts (any type of account), make sure there is not an open balance left. This includes accounts like with the cable company and cell phone.

CHAPTER - 10

RE-ESTABLISHING YOUR CREDIT

The road to reestablishing your credit can be a bumpy one, especially if you have to start over from scratch. The main thing you want to remember is that you need to have a solid foundation to rebuild your reputation. Several basic guidelines can help you to stay on course.

Whatever your goals are, once your credit report has gotten the boost that it needs, the efforts to reestablish your credit should begin with you. While you may have big dreams, you need to recover slowly. You don't want to make a misstep and end up falling back down the rabbit hole again.

Often, after having a rough bout with credit, the tendency is to swear off credit for good. The vow to go strictly cash can be healthy after surviving a difficult time with creditors and bill collectors. However, that is not always a wise decision. In fact, it could make it even more difficult for you later on. You've learned your lesson about bad credit, but you are smarter now, and you know that credit itself is not the bad guy, it's how you use it.

You now have a credit goal, and you know what to do with it. You know how much credit you can charge and still keep your score high, and you know the importance of making timely payments. You have all the tools you need in your arsenal to start your rebuilding campaign.

Step 1: Know How Much Credit You Need

This will give you a general idea of just how much credit you should have.

For this, you need to determine your debt to income ratio. When you are ready to apply for new credit, lenders will look at this percentage to make a final decision on giving you credit.

The formula for this is simple. Take you're the total from your list of financial obligations and divide it by your gross monthly income. It will give you the percentage of credit you should have in your arsenal. For example, if your monthly income is $1500.00 and your total monthly expenses is $800, the formula should look something like this.

800/1500 = 53%

The higher this percentage is, the less likely a

creditor will be willing to issue you knew credit, even with a good score.

Step 2: Start Small

You may have big dreams but keep it within realistic boundaries. Remember, you're trying to recover from credit illness. If you had been physically ill to the point where you needed hospitalization, you wouldn't come home from the hospital and automatically resume your same routine. You will build up your strength a little at a time until you were back to the same physical condition you were before.

You should view rebuilding your credit in the same way. Don't look to establish an unsecured bank credit card fresh out of the gate. These are probably the most difficult to get.

When filling out your application, here are a few things to keep in mind to make the process go smoother and the results will lean more in your favor.

Do not put in more than three applications for credit in a single month. More than that and your score will drop.

Don't add anything to your application that won't benefit you in some way. Some businesses will allow you to make purchases without established credit but will only report to the credit bureau once you've paid it off. Only put these on your application if you've made regular payments and you know it will boost your score.

Only apply to those that will raise your overall credit score.

As the months go by and you are making regular payments, you can begin to increase your purchase amounts little by little. Your creditor will notice that you are spending wisely and will likely drop the need for a security behind the card you have and perhaps even increase your limit. Remember, they make their money by charging interest so the more money you borrow, the more they can earn. Still, you don't have credit to support them, so maintain self-control and stay within your limits and your score will naturally increase.

Step 3: Protect What You Have

No matter how much or how little credit you have, never take it for granted. Make sure that you follow the rules and your credit should stay in good condition.

With revolving credit (credit cards), avoid using them too often. Only charge as much as you can reasonably pay off within a given month. No doubt, you will continue to hit rough patches here and there, even people with good credit need to be prepared. With credit that you use infrequently, make it a habit of making a small purchase from time to time so that the account does not become inactive. Then pay off the total balance immediately when you do.

Establish a rapport with your creditors. That way, if you end up paying late one month, you have a friend you can call that can help you to recover quickly. Missing a payment or paying late can be the death knell for a newly recovered credit score, the more friends you have in your corner, the more likely you will come out on top when that happens.

Use automation when you can. We all live busy lives, and it can be easy for a date to pass by without noticing it. One way to do this is to use modern technology to your advantage by taking advantage of automated payment systems. This will ensure that every payment will be made on time without you having to worry about it.

There are several ways to do this.

It is pretty easy to make up automatic payment arrangements through any of these plans but arranging it directly with your creditor is probably the fastest and most straightforward way to do it.

A word of caution; if you decide to make this arrangement through your bank, you will always have to make sure that your account has a sufficient balance to make the payment. This can start an ugly domino effect that could threaten to undermine all the efforts you've made to get your credit back on top.

This decision works best for those who have a regular monthly income that they can be sure will be in their bank at the right time. At the end of the day, the main goal is never to be late or miss a payment so you can avoid falling behind and running into a lot more problems than you bargained for.

You're in It for the Long Haul

When you're under a lot of pressure from collection agencies and creditors, it is easy to think that repairing credit and getting back on track is an emergency, but your credit will be with you for the long-term. There will be some things you won't be able to address immediately, and you will have to wait it out.

Don't rush the process but instead, take your time, be methodical in your approach, and the chances of your clearing up your good name are quite good.

Focus on the future, not the immediate present, and you will be driven to make sure that every step you take will be sustainable and you will be able to establish and maintain your new credit score for years to come.

CHAPTER - 11

SIMPLE TIPS/ FAQ ABOUT CREDIT REPAIR

Phew! It's been a long talk. I have mentioned practically everything you need to know. But I shouldn't bring this to a close without offering you some invaluable tips that can be easily remembered and practiced in your daily transactions. Applying them will make it a lot easier to handle your debts and fix your credit repairs. I hope by now you see clearly that you honestly have no use for credit repair companies at any phase. You may use a credit counselor many times, but yes, this is something you can fix on your own.

So, what the tips for fixing your credit efficiently?

1.   Keep your eye on your credit reports: Your credit report is the quickest pointer to the state of your finance. Since it contains the vital data that can determine your employment, chances of obtaining a loan, et cetera, you can make a lot of progress if you keep an eye on it. You want to

know when something is not about right. When you are starting to lax in your transaction with a credit union et cetera. You can make informed decisions and calculations if you are up to date with your credit situation.

2.   Keep   records   and   documents: Documentation can save your face in several situations. If you keep your records promptly and adequately, you will effortlessly realize the instant errors occur on your report. You also have enough shreds of evidence to back your claims anywhere. If you suck at documentation, you will be helpless when credit unions try to pull a fast one on you. You may think that is not likely, but the reality is that sometimes, they deliberately manipulate the figures. If you have got no records of receipts, transaction data et al., it becomes hard to prove them wrong. You may even assume you are the problem.

3.   Dispute when you have to: From the last page, you can tell that credit unions may be surprisingly tricky. Credit Bureaus are lagging too. It appears that the only person who has your interests in their heart is you. So, take up the job of proofreading the final reports all the time. Try to make all your disputes at once. But if you can't, you should harbor no estimation, and dispute as many records you don't agree with on your profile.

4.   Play when you can win: Just like credit unions would pull a fast one on you at every opportunity, you can launch the offensive too. You only have to be strategic, do not fight off an item until you are doubly sure that your creditor or information provider cannot defend that information. Whether the debt was real or not, you have a chance of taking it off-limits.

5.   Higher Credit Limits, Lower Credit Utilization: Make it a job to always improve your credit limits. At the same time, widen the margin between your credit limit and your credit utilization. Remember that this simple trick is enough to win 30% of your credit score if FICO was ever gone by. The other scoring models do not underrate this margin either.

6.   Get some unused credit cards: here is another fast way to improve your credit score. You may get new credit cards and drop them in a box. You are not going to use them at all, but with them, you have expanded your credit limit and at a little extra cost. Perhaps, your annual maintenance fee. If just a bit more, this is a proven method that can help you get rank better when credit utilization is considered.

7.   Include your utilities when you can: Now that you know your credit bureaus are ready to boost your credit report with your utilities, it makes perfect sense to get your phone bills,

rent, and as many as you can into your credit reports. Be quick to remember; you are doing this only if you don't owe these companies. You don't want to make things any harder on yourself.

8.   Pay promptly: Paying promptly can't be overstressed. People give out funds on the understanding that you are entirely reliable. So do companies, organizations, and every entity that has considered you for a loan at any time. It follows suit that you should keep your part of the deal. If you have to set a reminder, or lend from elsewhere to fix this loan and extend the time you have got, do it!

9.   Hang on a better friend: There is always a better friend around, it could help to hang on their coattail sometimes too. If you are lucky to have anyone with an impressive record willing to sign you on, you should ensure you don't throw their trust in the thrash too. They kept their profile by being principled and consistent. Don't drag them into circumstances they were not set to handle.

10.   Use just what you need: As much as the use of credit cards and many revolving loans are tempting, you should strictly use just what you need. It helps to be principled and picky in a purchase. It is hard to walk into a store and find attractive garbs or portfolios and still

control yourself from plucking them when you can simply do it, use your credit card, and pay at leisure. The reality is that poor buying decisions can lead to unimaginably high debts.

Frequently Asked Questions

What are the three credit bureaus?

If you can erase an item from your records, does it wipe off the debt?

That's a doubled-edged question. It depends on the situation on your hand. You may be able to wipe debt off your records because your creditor is willing to withdraw that data and settle the debts with you, outside your credit reports. In this case, your debts remain intact, so erasing items doesn't wipe your debts.

In another case, you may have got an item out because your creditor or information provider doesn't have enough proof that the debt is yours. If it gets crossed out eventually, you are absolved of further payments. So, erasing that item gets that item out here.

Why should I get reports from the three bureaus?

That's how best you can get an all-round collection of information. It is often the case that the credit bureaus gather facts from different sources. Hence, what you find in one may be missing in the others. In most cases, TransUnion has more data than the two others. Still, you should get reports from these three and compare them.

Can I use a credit repair company?

Sure, you can! But I strongly recommend you save the extra bucks. This is pretty easy and straightforward. Technology has made it easier still. This book contains the guides you may need at any stage that you need to fix your credits. You may also contact a credit bureau for support.

How long does it take to fix errors on a card?

If your request isn't disregarded, your credit bureau starts an investigation and rounds it up in 30 days. In two weeks more, you get the results of their investigations. So, it takes 45 days on approximate.

Can I simply restart?

That's suicidal! Trying to start a new credit profile is proof that you are trying to be unreal. You are shying away from reality. You are trying to avoid claiming responsibility for your wrongdoings. It is considered a crime. So, drop the idea already, please.

CHAPTER - 12

THE TOP 10 NEGATIVE INFLUENCERS OF YOUR CREDIT SCORE

1 .Collections Accounts

Collections occur when you have a debt that you have not paid in a timely manner. When you fall substantially behind in delinquency on a bill like a credit card or medical bill, the original creditor will usually write off the debt as a total loss. They then sell it out to a collection agency. It is then entirely up to the collection agency to try to get the money that you owe back.

Not every lender or creditor has the same policy on this action. A great number of credit cards send out the 180-day delinquent accounts to collectors. At this point, either they or the collection agency will report your account as "in collections" to the major three credit bureaus. This will cause you to have a "collection" notation on your credit reports.

The original creditor may or may not alert you

to the fact that they are sending your account out to collections.

Once you suffer an in-collection account on your credit report, you can anticipate your credit score plunging. The number of points such a collection account will impact your score depends on how high your credit score proves to be when it becomes reported as a collection account.

A correspondingly higher credit score will lose more points in general.

The amount of the account in collection will also determine how big an impact this status has on your credit score. If your original debt amount was under $100, the collection account may appear on your credit reports but not much harm your score (or even hurt it at all with Vantage Scoring's model for under $250 collections accounts).

2. Foreclosures And Short Sales

Foreclosures and short sales have to do with mortgages on which you fall behind. The bank has the right to foreclose on your property if you become seriously delinquent. You could also arrange a short sale with the bank to repay part of the loan and settle it. Both of these impacts your credit score in several meaningful ways.

Yet short sales done properly will create a less negative effect on your personal credit score than an all-out foreclosure will.

Foreclosures can have a devastating impact on your credit score. For starters, it will stay on your credit report for a full 10 years, though the impact will be gradually less as it gets older.

The late payments that led to the foreclosure cause a significant negative effect on your credit score. According to FICO, foreclosures will cause an estimated drop of from 175 to 300 points in your score2.

Short sales have a considerably smaller impact on your score. This is a more difficult procedure as it requires approval from the mortgage lender who is involved. You will have to give the lender an application detailed with information on your financials.

If you can arrange a short sale with your lender without missing any mortgage payments, it will reduce the negative impact on your credit score.

If you cannot get a fast approval of such a short sale from your lender, you may be forced into missing payments on your mortgage. This would cause your score more harm as timely payment history amounts to 35 percent of your FICO credit scoring component. The lender could also determine that you do not meet their qualifications for a short sale, which would then leave you with either finding a way to hold onto the house or letting it fall into foreclosure eventually.

3. Bill Payment History Of Late Payments

There is no larger single element that impacts your credit score than timely payments (amounting to 35 percent of your credit scoring model). This means that missing a payment and having it marked as late to the credit reporting bureaus will hurt, sometimes quite a lot.

A late payment that is reported as 30 days or more past due could crash your credit score by up to 100 points.

If your credit is without blemish, it might cause this amount of a drop. When your score is already lower, it will not affect it as much, but it will still damage it3.

4. Increased Debt To Credit Ratio

The total debt that you possess remains the second largest factor in determining your personal credit score. As a 30 percent component of your credit score, you can not afford to abuse this ratio. Credit scoring models look at this credit utilization (the ratio of your credit card balance to your total credit limit) on every one of your cards as well as your total credit utilization for all accounts.

The higher these balances are compared to your credit limits, the more damage this does to your personal score.

The worst possible thing you can show in this category is over limit or maxed out card balances (amounting to 100 percent or higher utilization).

Remember that credit scores also consider the proximity of your loan balances to original loan amounts. This is why paying down loan balances will help your credit score.

The opposite is true too. If you carry large amounts of debt (in particular credit card debt), this will harm your credit score and be damaging in your efforts to get new loans and credit card approvals (or to increase your credit limits).

5. Repossessions

Repossession occurs if you miss multiple loan payments that cause you to default on your car loan. Repossession is an especially bad mark on a credit report as it remains for up to seven years and can cause you a 100-point credit score drop.

Repossessions Sharm your credit in three meaningful ways.

This starts with late payments. These cause negative effects on your credit report for up to seven years by themselves. Once your car has been repossessed, the three main credit bureaus will likely include notations that your car has been repossessed for up to seven long years.

Collections efforts to recover money you still owe on the loan after they repossess and sell your vehicle will also show on your report for as long as seven years. This is the case even if you pay off the debt later.

6. Negative Narratives

According to Vantage Score, negative narratives are notations on your credit report that are derogatory. These cause the most harm and will keep your score from rising for longer time frames. Lenders consider such derogatory entries to be proof of debt that you mismanaged. It explains why the various credit scoring models count them as sufficient reason to allow significant and lasting reductions to your credit score.

You should avoid all of these 12 derogatory remarks if at all possible:

7. Third Party Collections

As one of your accounts reaches the seriously delinquent point, the creditor may cut their losses by selling off the account to a third-party collection agency. This could happen after they have made numerous attempts through their own internal collections department. After they have sold off your account to the third party, this in collection account can get reported on your credit report as a separate delinquent account.

This is part of the way that they create substantial negative effects on your credit scores.

Third party collections only appear on accounts that are unsecured (like personal loans or credit cards). Mortgages, car loans, and other secured loans show up as foreclosures or repossessions on your report. Repossessed car loans can also be sent out for third party collection. If your car is repossessed then sold at a steep discount at auction, then the recovered amount could be lower than your remaining balance, which would then be sent out for collections.

There are only two ways to have collections taken off of your credit report.

If the information reported is valid, it takes a full seven years from the first delinquency date for the information to drop off of your three reports. This delinquency date is the point from which your account first went delinquent (and you never again made it current).

If the information on collections is not accurate, you can always file disputes with the credit reporting bureau. This would result in the record either being removed or updated if the credit bureau rules that the dispute in your favor7.

8. The Age Of Your Credit History

The age of your credit history could be a positive or a negative influencer of your credit. Lenders consider this length of time to ascertain the chances of your repaying your loan or credit in a timely fashion. With a longer history, this demonstrates to them that you possess more experience exercising and managing credit successfully.

The theory goes that the longer amount of credit history you have, the more certain lenders are able to be in deciding the quantity of risk they are assuming in lending you money.

Opening or even closing an account can lower your credit score over the short term.

This is because it will reduce the average age of your credit accounts. If you close an existing credit account that has a longer credit history, this will likely cause a negative impact to your scores. This impact becomes more pronounced should you decide to close out a number of older accounts at a single time, per Vantage Score.

Opening new accounts waters down your length of credit history and can similarly cost you points, particularly if you open several new accounts in close proximity to one another8.

9. Payday Loans

In general, Payday Loans do not negatively impact your credit score so long as you pay them back fully and in a timely manner. There could be an exception. Some lenders may regard Payday Loans as negative since they feel that customers of these loans are not as reliable a borrower as others. In such cases, having a Payday Loan on your personal credit history could harm your chances of getting approved for some loans.

It is important to keep in mind that you have more than a single credit score. The two major models of FICO and Vantage Score, as well as the three main credit reporting bureaus of Experian, Equifax, and TransUnion, all calculate scores differently using their own proprietary criteria.

The result is that Payday Loans can impact your various scores differently. Some lenders also do not distinguish between traditional loans and Payday Loans9.

10. Unemployment

The personal information section of your credit report may list past or current employers. This is not promised to be a complete employment history or picture. Instead it is an employer list that was included in your past applications for credit that then reached the three main credit reporting bureaus (from your lenders).

This information is only obtained when you apply for a loan or credit, and not all lenders even report it. This explains why any employer list is not likely to be comprehensive. There are likely to be gaps shown in such an employment list (which depends on the last time you applied for credit).

The good news is that this will not create any impact on your credit history or score.

In fact, unemployment will never directly impact your credit scores. The reason is that your credit reports are not set up to prove if you are employed. Instead, they share information related to debt and credit.

CHAPTER - 13

THE RIGHT MINDSET

Many folks suffer a financial crisis at some point. They may have to deal with overspending, loss of a job, a family member or personal illness. These financial problems can be and usually are, overwhelming. To make these situations worse, most people don't even know where to begin to solve these financial dilemmas. Our goal here is to shine some light on the strategies to help get youth Accumulating basic consumer debt will chain you into slavery and you could possibly spend your life held down by your own obligations to repay these loans. Who do you work for? I don't care what you say; the real answer is your creditors if you are currently stuck paying debt. There are many forms of "dumb debt" you can get trapped into. We are all sold images and lifestyles hundreds of times per day to provoke this materialistic behavior. The person or institution lending you the money is trusting that you have the ability to hold up your end of the bargain, basically. Sometimes, it may seem impossible to live your life without the option to get a credit, but this is what bad credit eventually leads to.

But how do you get a credit in the first place? What is the process you have to go through to loan money? Well, it all starts with a credit application to a bank or some other party that has the necessary finances. Your application is reviewed and, if they think there won't be a problem with getting their money back, you sign a contract and get your money in no time. The application you submit to a lender is used to obtain a credit report from one or several reporting agencies, depending on how much money you need. These two documents are given scores and, if your score is enough, you'll get the money you need. If not, your application will be rejected. If you don't fall into any of these categories, then a judgment call has to be made by the person or institution providing the credit. The more "good credit" criteria you meet, the more likely it is that you will get your credit.

However, there are several things that you must consider before you put yourself into the category of citizens unaffected by bad credit. First of all, the lenders look for certain things in your application, such as an up to date credit report and no late payments on your other financial obligations. They are interested to see if you've had a job for more than a year and have a stable income, as well as a stable residence. They also evaluate the situation of your utility and phone bills and appreciate if you include information about additional credit cards or other types of cards. It is not only banks and money lenders that look at this type of information. Sometimes, if you want to get a new job, your employer will conduct this type of research too, so maintaining a good credit is crucial in these troubled times we live in.

What type of credit should you get? That depends on what you plan to do with the money. The most used types of credit are secured and signature credits. For smaller loans, there's no need for that, as no institution would like to end up with a store of household items, so they lend you money or issue a credit card in your name simply based on the strength of your credit so far.

There is hope; you as the borrower have many options to get rid of debt. You can take advantage of budgeting and other techniques, such as debt consolidation, debt settlement, credit counseling, and bankruptcy procedures. You just have to choose the best strategy that will work for you. When choosing from the various options, you have to consider your debt level, your discipline, and plans for the future.

The Good Debt

Some people find it hard to live debt free at least they will have some debt to pay off. While some debts are discouraged, good debt is considered as the money you borrow so that you can pay for things that you really need or things that increase in value. On the flip side, bad debt is one that arises from things that you only want and often decrease in value.

Of course, debt isn't a bad thing; it's just how you use the money that matters.

For a good debt, you will always have a good reason to justify it, and a developed plan for paying it so that you can clear the debt as quickly as possible.

An individual with good debt will also have the cheapest methods of borrowing money. They will do this by looking at the borrowing method, rate of interest, credit amount, and charges that are appropriate to them.

Sometimes, it may imply a deal with the least possible interest rate, but sometimes, it may not.

Examples of good debt

Paying for medical care. There is no fixed amount of money to borrow to ensure your loved one stays healthy. You can manage to pay off the money you borrow, but it is impossible to replace a human life. If a person requires expensive treatments to ensure they remain healthy, this would be an acceptable debt, no matter what.

Borrow money for education. When you apply for a student loan debt, you aren't making a wrong decision. In general, people with college degrees earn more income in their life than those without a degree.

And applying for a student loan so that you can support the education of your child defeats the idea of using your savings. After all, you cannot borrow money to pay for your savings. Multiple government programs provide low-interest student loans, and you can always cut student loan interest on your taxes.

Taking out a mortgage on a home. Taking a loan of this amount can be overwhelming, but purchasing a house creates ownership in something that will house you, and generate some retirement money. Even while you struggle to clear your debt, you may consider it an advantage to put any available liquid cash as a deposit, though it may not be the right choice.

A home mortgage interest is cut on your taxes, and the rate of interest is lower on your home loan than on the credit card. In other words, it is important to have money to pay for other expenses instead of credit.

Though purchasing a house was initially considered a strong, future-proof investment, certain homeowners do find themselves on the wrong side on their home mortgage loan. They owe banks more than the value of their homes. However, strategic planning, purchasing only what you can afford, and maintaining low interest by having good credit may allow you to purchase a home that one day you will own completely.

Buying a car. If you don't have public transport in your area, or you cannot manage to get someone with whom you can carpool with, then you may have to consider buying a car. An auto loan can either be "good" or "bad", but the main thing is to ensure that the auto loan is a good debt, so look for the lowest possible rates on your loan. In addition, you need to make a large down payment while ensuring that you remain with some cash on hand just in case you need it.

Your best goal should be to go for a used car model instead of a brand-new one, possibly saving yourself thousands on the sticker price and the interest that is paid throughout the loan.

Business loans. While this may not be seen

as good debt, borrowing money to begin a business or expand a business is perhaps a great idea if the business is thriving. After all, you need money to make more money, right?

Sometimes, you may have to borrow capital to employ new people, purchase a new device, pay for advertisement, or even develop the first new widget you designed. The point is that you borrow this money to expand the business or increase income, then this will count as good debt.

What is Bad Debt?

Bad debt is that which depletes your wealth and isn't affordable. Plus, it provides no means to pay for itself.

Bad debts may have no realistic repayment plans and usually deplete when people buy things at an impulse. If you aren't sure whether you can repay the money, then don't borrow the money because that will be a bad debt.

Examples of bad debt

The credit card debt. A typical household in the United States has a balance of more than $10,000 on their credit card every month. However, the debt usually increases faster than we may realize and is always used to purchase things that we want instead of need. It is easier to think that you can afford something using a card than paying it with cash.

Borrowing from a 401K. When you ask for money from a 401K program, you will need to chat with the IRS, and if you aren't using the money to purchase a home, you will need to pay the loan in five years. If you fail to pay it back, you risk being charged with a severe penalty. Also, the interest that you pay on the loan will get taxed twice.

You can't get a loan to fund your retirement. For that reason, borrowing money from your retirement plan to use it to pay for anything that isn't part of retirement is a bad idea. You will be putting your retirement at risk when you get a loan from a 401k, so don't make this mistake.

Payday loans. It may appear easy to borrow money from payday loan firms, but it is hard to pay it back. These companies offer loans with very high interest rates. The companies take advantage of the fact that many people need that money. As a result, borrowing a small amount may end up costing you a lot.

Payday loans aren't considered the worst kind of debt that you can take on. If you really need a short-term loan, it is better to go for a cash advance on a credit card rather than borrow money from these firms.

Using consolidation or settlement strategies to pay down debts.

Debt consolidation is another strategy that can be used to manage your debts. It involves combining two or more debts at a lower interest rate than you are currently at.

But it is worth doing your research and making some phone calls to see if there is a company that's willing to work with you. If you can lower your monthly bill to a manageable level, at an interest rate that's reasonable, that can make all the difference in handling your debt.

Like many strategies, you have had the option of settling your debts with companies for decades. Lenders always want as much money as you can give them versus being shafted for the entire amount in a bankruptcy. It is just that consolidation and settlement options rose in popularity during the recent financial crisis making it appear in more articles and news pieces than ever before.

CHAPTER - 14

RATING AGENCIES

Who Are the Rating Agencies?

Contrary to what the term "agency" might suggest, these are private for-profit organizations and not regulatory or government organizations.

The rating agencies' business model is based primarily on remuneration paid by rated entities, advisory activities and the dissemination of rating data.

What Is The Notation?

The rating gives an opinion on the ability of an issuer to meet its obligations to its creditors, or security to generate payments of principal and interest in accordance with the schedule. The rating may also relate not to an issuer in general, but to a security (bond, ABS, and MBS, etc.) in particular. The rating of securitization operations expanded considerably before the 2008-2009 financial crisis.

What Does The Notation, Not Say?

Agencies insist a lot on the fact that rating is an opinion, not some form of guarantee or commitment on their part, which under US law shelters them from lawsuits from investors.

The rating is an assessment of credit risk to the exclusion of all other risks. It gives no indication of the potential profitability of an investment, nor the volatility of securities issued. The rating does not say anything about the liquidity of a security, that is to say, the possibility of finding a price and a market counterparty to buy or sell this security. This aspect was badly felt during the last financial crisis when many investors were unable to liquidate their positions on securities rated "triple A".

The Rating Processes

The rating is generally established at the request of the issuer, but it can also be triggered by the rating agency itself.

The objective is to determine what amount of credit enhancement is required for each tranche to achieve the desired rating.

As in the rating of issuers, the agency continues to monitor the rated security after having published its initial rating, especially the behavior of collateral pool in the face of economic conditions and may need to review the rating.

The Role Of Rating Agencies In The Financial System

In fact, ratings are widely used in the regulatory framework on the one hand, and also in the strategies of many investors.

To be eligible for central bank refinancing operations, the securities must have a minimum rating.

Similarly, the management objectives of many investors are based on ratings: for example, a UCITS (Undertakings for Collective Investments in Transferable Securities) may have in its objectives to hold 80% of assets issued by issuers rated at least "BBB". The indicators for monitoring credit risk in corporate and investment banks are also based on ratings.

Rating Agencies And The Financial Crisis

Rating agencies are accused of participating in the outbreak of the 2007-2009 financial crisis for two reasons. First of all, they tended to note too much complacently titles that eventually turned out to be "toxic", despite (or because of?) The sophisticated financial packages on which they rested. When real estate market conditions began to deteriorate in the United States, they reacted by sharply lowering the rating of many issues ("downgrading"), contributing to the downward spiral in which the market was driven.

The agencies had already aroused criticism during bankruptcies that they had been totally unable to anticipate: Parmalat, Enron, WorldCom, etc. Subsequently, they were again singled out during the Greek debt crisis.

CONCLUSION

Beginning up company is one concept you might not even welcome in the first hand. You may be thinking of the risk included when putting up some capital for your business. .

However, despite of these fears of losing, it is constantly good to consider some of the reasons why you must be operating. While dangers are present, nevertheless, it takes an effort in your part to make your organization success realized. Here are some of the reasons you must make your own business:

Frequently, the reason why the majority of us take our jobs as problems is because of the reality that we are reporting to a bossy remarkable or we have to deliver something which our bossy exceptional would like us to do. With those continuous need, in some cases, you may wind up losing your job particularly when your boss does not like your efficiency. In the end, your lifeline is held by your employer than yourself. Would you choose to offer some leverage in your lifeline by being a boss to yourself? For this reason, starting up a small business for your own is one method of putting yourself in control.

No More Urgent and ASAP deadlines! The most dreaded word that employees usually encounter are the words "Urgent' and "ASAP". Often, these are reasons of bossy superiors who have actually not delegated the job on time. In this way, you can have the liberty with your schedule and move freely based in your pace.

Beginning up your organization is the other way. When you put in more effort in marketing your item and you offer more, you will be getting more revenues. For this reason, the more you will be encouraged to work for it.

Possibly among the finest thing to startup your own organization is that you will be doing the important things you really want to do. For this reason, it is constantly good to get the benefit of doing your own thing as you will no longer consider it as work but more of enjoying what you will do. The majority of people who will be thinking about work as something they would cherish are more likely to be successful.

Try to concentrate your efforts first in succeeding your service in little scale. As you attempt to see the success of your small company, put some capital for expansion. There you will be having those terrific chances of making it huge! If you've currently created your own business however sometimes question why you ever took the plunge then let this be a suggestion of why you made the ideal decision.

Taking Control! Then you'll appreciate how little control you truly have over what you do, if you've ever had a 9-5 job. As an entrepreneur you have supreme control of what you do, why and when, which is really empowering. If things don't go to prepare you likewise have no-one else to blame. You can and should pick a company which you're passionate about. If you don't simply chase after the cash, but rather select something you really take pleasure in then your day-to-day routine can feel more like a full-time hobby than genuine work.

Making a Difference! With your own service you can truly make a distinction and have a powerful impact in a niche which you're passionate about. You can add genuine worth to people's lives and do things the way you believe thy ought to be done. You don't have to compromise on worth, quality or service. You can deliver the very best. If you're in a little specialized niche you can quickly end up being identified as a thought leader, expert, top supplier or simply a leading guy/girl in your field. It's difficult to gain much acknowledgment for what you perform in a 9-5 job, however as an entrepreneur your impact is far reaching.

Even though the economy's unsteady at the minute it's still much easier than ever to start your own business. You can begin in your living space, in your spare time and with the cash you have in your pocket right now. Get your financial freedom today by starting a small business in 2020.